Meet the Quokkas!

By Caryn Jenner

US Senior Editor Shannon Beatty
US Editor Jane Perlmutter
Senior Editor Carrie Love
Project Editor Kritika Gupta
Art Editors Mohd Zishan, Polly Appleton
Jacket Co-ordinator Issy Walsh
Jacket Designer Dheeraj Arora
DTP Designers Dheeraj Singh, Nand Kishore Acharya
Project Picture Researcher Sakshi Saluja
Producer, pre-production Tony Phipps
Senior producer Ena Matagic
Managing Editors Penny Smith, Monica Saigal
Deputy Managing Art Editor Ivy Sengupta
Managing Art Editor Mabel Chan
Delhi Team Head Malavika Talukder
Publishing Manager Francesca Young
Creative Director Helen Senior
Publishing Director Sarah Larter

Reading Consultant Dr. Barbara Marinak
Subject Consultant Kim Bryan

First American Edition, 2020
Published in the United States by DK Publishing
1450 Broadway, Suite 801, New York, New York 10018

A catalog record for this book is available from the Library of Congress.
ISBN: 978-1-4654-9319-4 (Paperback)
ISBN: 978-1-4654-9320-0 (Hardcover)

DK books are available at special discounts when purchased in bulk for sales promotions,
premiums, fund-raising, or educational use. For details, contact: DK Publishing Special Markets,
1450 Broadway, Suite 801, New York, New York 10018
SpecialSales@dk.com

Printed and bound in China

The publisher would like to thank the following for their kind permission to reproduce their photographs:
(Key: a-above; b-below/bottom; c-center; f-far; l-left; r-right; t-top)
1 Dreamstime.com: Kitchner Bain. **3 Dreamstime.com:** Ashley Whitworth (br). **4–5 Getty Images:** Sarah Lewis / Moment RF.
6–7 Dreamstime.com: Adwo. **8 Dreamstime.com:** Alfotokunst (br); Oliver Neumann (c). **9 Getty Images:** Posnov.
10 Dreamstime.com: Johnny Lye. **11 Alamy Stock Photo:** Avalon / Photoshot License (b). **12 iStockphoto.com:** J_Knaupe (b).
14 Dreamstime.com: Lizgiv (bl); Wiritjiribin (br). **15 iStockphoto.com:** JohnCarnemolla. **16 Dreamstime.com:** Andrey Moisseyev.
17 Alamy Stock Photo: Gekko Studios. **18–19 Alamy Stock Photo:** mauritius images GmbH. **20 Alamy Stock Photo:** Frans
Lanting Studio. **21 Alamy Stock Photo:** Bill Bachman (cla). **Dreamstime.com:** Artistrobd (cr). **SuperStock:** Animals Animals (clb).
23 Alamy Stock Photo: Avico Ltd. **24 SuperStock:** Kevin Schafer / Minden Pictures (t). **25 naturepl.com:** Kevin Schafer. **26–27
Alamy Stock Photo:** Avalon / Photoshot License. **28 Alamy Stock Photo:** Kitch Bain (b). **29 Dreamstime.com:** Peter Galleghan
(t). **30 Dreamstime.com:** Ozflash (b). **31 naturepl.com:** Kevin Schafer. **32–33 Alamy Stock Photo:** Avalon / Photoshot License.
34 Alamy Stock Photo: Avalon / Photoshot License (b). **35 Getty Images:** John Crux Photography. **36–37 Alamy Stock Photo:**
Angus McComiskey. **38 Dreamstime.com:** Barbro Rutgersson. **39 iStockphoto.com:** Totajla (b). **40 Getty Images:** Greg Wood /
AFP (b). **41 Getty Images:** Schafer & Hill. **42 Dreamstime.com:** Tmyra (clb). **43 Dreamstime.com:** Adam9277 (cl); David Steele (tr, br).

Endpapers: Front: **Alamy Stock Photo:** Avalon / Photoshot License. Back: **Alamy Stock Photo:** Avalon / Photoshot License.

Cover images: Front: **Dreamstime.com:** Oliver Neumann c; Back: **Dreamstime.com:** Lizgiv cla.x

All other images © Dorling Kindersley
For further information see: www.dkimages.com

For the curious

www.dk.com

Contents

Chapter 1
Meet the quokkas

Look at these animals. Do you see the smiles on their furry faces?

These animals are quokkas [KWOK-ahs]. A quokka looks like it is smiling because the ends of its mouth turn up. That's why quokkas are called the happiest animals in the world.

Quokkas are mammals that live in Australia.

A quokka is about the size of a house cat. It has a chubby body with thick, brown fur. Its tail is thin, like a rat's tail.

A quokka has big back paws and small front paws. Watch out! It also has sharp claws.

Quokkas can weigh up to 9 lbs (4.2 kg).

A quokka's face looks friendly.
Its ears are round like a teddy bear's
ears. It has dark eyes and a big,
black nose. Plus there's the happy
quokka smile!

Quokkas spend most
of their time in bushes
and undergrowth.

A joey stays in its mother's pouch for up to six and a half months.

A female quokka has a
special pouch on her tummy.
This is where she keeps her baby.
A baby quokka is called a joey.
See the little joey peeking out
of its pouch? Peep!

Quokkas usually have one baby at a time,
but sometimes they have twins.

Where do quokkas live?

Quokkas live in Australia. Most quokkas now live on Rottnest Island off the coast of Australia. There aren't many quokkas left on the mainland.

Rottnest Island is home to about 10,000 quokkas.

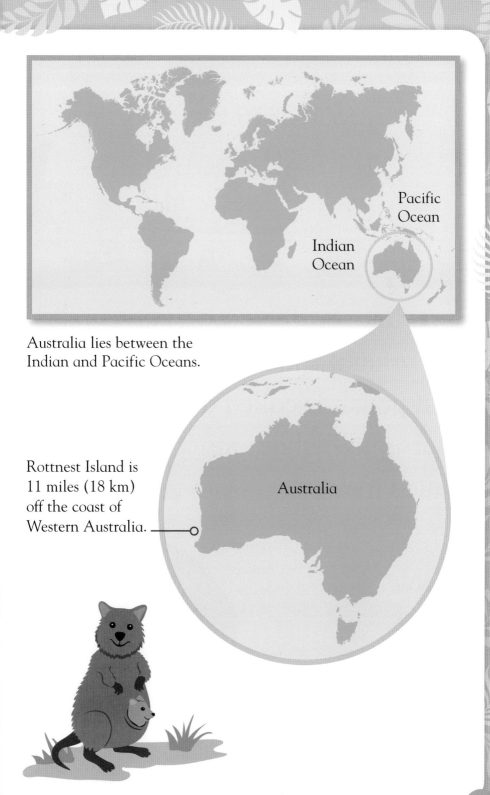

Australia lies between the Indian and Pacific Oceans.

Rottnest Island is 11 miles (18 km) off the coast of Western Australia.

Pacific Ocean

Indian Ocean

Australia

Chapter 2
Pals with pouches

An animal that keeps its baby
in a pouch is called a marsupial.
Marsupial babies are
called joeys.

Red-necked
wallaby

Quokka

What other animals keep their joeys in a pouch? Wallabies and kangaroos do. A quokka is a kind of wallaby. Kangaroos and wallabies live in Australia.

Red kangaroo

A koala sitting
on a branch
with its joey

Other marsupials
from Australia
are koalas and
wombats. Koalas live
in trees. Wombats dig
underground homes.

16

A mother wombat keeps her
joey in a pouch near her tail.
The pouch faces backward.
That way it doesn't fill with
dirt when the mother is digging.

A common wombat mother curls up with its joey

Another kind of marsupial is the opossum. Opossums live in North and South America. A mother opossum takes care of lots of joeys in her pouch.

When the joeys grow too big for the pouch, they hold onto their mother's fur.

A Virginia opossum carrying babies on its back

Many marsupials

There are more than 330 different kinds of marsupials. Here are some of them.

Red kangaroo
A red kangaroo is the largest marsupial.

Numbat
A numbat catches insects with its long, sticky tongue.

Tasmanian devil
A Tasmanian devil makes an awful smell when it's stressed.

Water opossum
A water opossum is the only marsupial that can swim.

Chapter 3
Growing up

A newborn quokka joey is
only about the size of a raisin.
The tiny joey stays safe and
warm in its mother's pouch.
It feeds on its mother's milk. It
doesn't look like a quokka
until it gets older.

A young joey inside
its mother's pouch

Joey peeking out of its mother's pouch

Soon the quokka joey grows fur. It pokes its head out of its mother's pouch and looks around.

After about six months, the joey climbs out of the pouch for the first time. It's ready to explore!

After about eight months, the quokka joey grows too big for its mother's pouch. It can find its own food.

A quokka mother and baby on Rottnest Island, Australia

Soon it will be all grown up.
It may stay with its mother until it
is about 20 months old.

Chapter 4
Cute critters

Hop, hop, hop! Quokkas hop around on their big back paws. Sometimes, they move around on all four paws.

A quokka sleeping with its head between its legs

Quokkas are usually active at night. During the day, they find shelter from the hot sun. They fall asleep in the shade.

Quokkas eat grass and leaves, and stems of shrubs and bushes. They climb up small bushes and trees. They pull down the branches with their sharp claws and eat the leaves.

Sometimes, there is no food. Then the quokka gets energy from fat stored in its tail.

Quokka eating a leaf

Quokkas live near streams and swamps. They drink the water. They also get water from the plants they eat.

A quokka jumps across a stream

Sometimes, quokkas make trails to help them get from place to place.

The quokkas on Rottnest Island live near people. Visitors come to the island especially to see the quokkas. They take a lot of photos. Quokkas are not afraid of people. They are friendly creatures, but they are still wild animals. They might bite!

Quokkas being photographed by a visitor

Chapter 5
Quokka survival

About 10,000 quokkas live on the small island of Rottnest. These lucky quokkas don't have to worry about other animals hunting them. That is one reason there are so many.

Quokkas are very popular on Rottnest Island. Since quokkas are wild, people are not allowed to touch them or feed them.

The plants and animals on Rottnest Island are protected by law.

Foxes are not native to Australia. They were taken to the country in the mid-1800s to be hunted.

There used to be a lot of quokkas on mainland Australia, too. Sadly, there aren't many left there now. Animals such as foxes and cats hunt them. People build roads and buildings on the quokkas' habitat and destroy it. Large wildfires also destroy the quokkas' habitat.

Quokkas have lost much of their habitat on mainland Australia due to wildfires and deforestation.

Quokkas are in danger of dying out on mainland Australia. People there are trying to help the quokkas. They are protecting the quokkas' habitat so it doesn't completely disappear. Hopefully, the quokkas will keep smiling for a long time to come.

An orphaned quokka joey in Australia

Quick quokka facts

Quokkas belong to the "macropod" animal family. Macropod means "big foot." Kangaroos are also macropods. Here are more quick quokka facts.

Quokkas live to be about ten years old in the wild.

Human food can make quokkas sick.

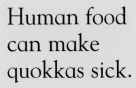

The name "quokka" is an Aboriginal word.

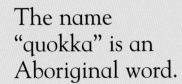

An explorer to Rottnest Island thought the quokkas were giant rats! He named the island Rottnest, meaning "rat's nest."

Quiz

1. Why does a quokka look like it's smiling?

2. How much does a quokka weigh?

3. What is a joey?

4. Where does a female quokka keep her baby?

5. Where do quokkas live?

6. Quokkas and koalas are marsupials. Can you name two other marsupials in this book?

7. When does a joey get too big to fit in its mother's pouch?

8. When are quokkas usually active?

9. Where does a quokka get energy from when it can't find food?

10. How many quokkas live on Rottnest Island?

Glossary

Aboriginal
Relating to the first people who lived in Australia.

deforestation
Cutting down trees over a large area by humans.

habitat
Where an animal or plant lives.

macropod
The family of animals that includes quokkas, wallabies, and kangaroos.

mammal
A warm-blooded animal that produces milk to feed its young.

marsupial
A type of mammal. Most females have a pouch in which their young live.

native
Relating to an animal or plant that occurs naturally in a place.

swamp
Low-lying wet ground also known as a bog.

Index

A LEVEL FOR EVERY READER

This book is a part of an exciting four-level reading series to support children in developing the habit of reading widely for both pleasure and information. Each book is designed to develop a child's reading skills, fluency, grammar awareness, and comprehension in order to build confidence and enjoyment when reading.

Ready for a Level 2 (Beginning to Read) book

A child should:

- be able to recognize a bank of common words quickly and be able to blend sounds together to make some words.
- be familiar with using beginner letter sounds and context clues to figure out unfamiliar words.
- sometimes correct his/her reading if it doesn't look right or make sense.
- be aware of the need for a slight pause at commas and a longer one at periods.

A valuable and shared reading experience

For many children, reading requires much effort, but adult participation can make reading both fun and easier. Here are a few tips on how to use this book with a young reader:

Check out the contents together:

- read about the book on the back cover and talk about the contents page to help heighten interest and expectation.
- discuss new or difficult words.
- talk about labels, annotations, and pictures.

Support the reader:

- give the book to the young reader to turn the pages.
- where necessary, encourage longer words to be broken into syllables, sound out each one, and then flow the syllables together; ask him/her to reread the sentence to check the meaning.
- encourage the reader to vary his/her voice as he/she reads; demonstrate how to do this if helpful.

Talk at the end of each book, or after every few pages:

- ask questions about the text and the meaning of the words used—this helps develop comprehension skills.
- read the quiz at the end of the book and encourage the reader to answer the questions, if necessary, by turning back to the relevant pages to find the answers.

Reading consultant: Dr. Barbara Marinak, Dean and Professor of Education at Mount St. Mary's University, Maryland.